THE VOICE

BY

MARGARET DELAND

ISBN - 978-93-5478-786-7

Design and setting By
Zinc Read
Email- zincread@gmail.com

Contents

Danny." William King grinned. Then he got up and, drawing his coat-tails forward, stood with his back to the jug of lilacs in Dr. Lavendar's fireplace. "Oh, well, of course it's all bosh," he said, and yawned; "I was on a case till four o'clock this morning," he apologized.

"William," said Dr. Lavendar, admiringly, "what an advantage you fellows have over us poor parsons! Everything a medical man doesn't understand is 'bosh'! Now, we can't classify things as easily as that."

"Well, I don't care," William said, doggedly; "from my point of view—"

"From your point of view," said Dr. Lavendar, "St. Paul was an epileptic, because he heard a Voice?"

"If you really want to know what I think—"

"I don't," Dr. Lavendar said; "I want you to know what I think. Mr. Roberts hasn't heard any Voice, yet; he is only listening for it. William, listening for the Voice of God isn't necessarily a sign of poor health; and provided a man doesn't set himself up to think he is the only person his Heavenly Father is willing to speak to, listening won't do him any harm. As for Henry Roberts, he is a humble old man. An example to me, William! I am pretty arrogant once in a while. I have to be, with such men as you in my congregation. No; the real trouble in that household is that girl of his. It isn't right for a young thing to live in such an atmosphere."

William agreed sleepily. "Pretty creature. Wish I had a daughter just like her," he said, and took himself off to make up for a broken night's rest. But Dr. Lavendar and Danny still sat in front of the lilac-filled fireplace, and thought of old Henry Roberts listening for the Voice of God, and of his Philippa. The father and daughter had lately taken a house on a road that wandered over the hills between elderberry-bushes and under sycamores, from Old Chester to Perryville. They were about half-way between the two little towns, and they did not seem to belong to either. Perryville's small manufacturing bustle repelled the silent old man whom Dr. Lavendar called an "Irvingite"; and Old Chester's dignity and dull aloofness repelled young Philippa. The result was that the Robertses and their one woman servant, Hannah, had been living on the Perryville pike for some months before anybody in either village was quite aware of their existence. Then one day in May, Dr. Lavendar's sagging old buggy pulled up at their gate, and the old minister called over the garden wall to Philippa: "Won't you give me some of your apple blossoms?"

That was the beginning of Old Chester's knowledge of the Roberts family. A little later Perryville came to know them, too: the Rev. John Fenn, pastor of the Perryville Presbyterian Church, got off his big, raw-boned Kentucky horse at the same little white gate in the brick wall at which Goliath had stopped, and walked solemnly—not noticing the apple blossoms—up to the porch. Henry Roberts was sitting there in the hot twilight, with a curious listening look in his face—a look of waiting expectation; it was so marked, that the caller involuntarily glanced over his shoulder to see if any other visitor was approaching; but there was nothing to be seen in the dusk but the roan nibbling at the hitching-post. Mr. Fenn said that he had called to inquire whether Mr. Roberts was a regular attendant at any place of worship. To which the old man replied gently that every place was a place of worship, and his own house was the House of God. John Fenn was honestly dismayed at such sentiments—dismayed, and a little indignant; and yet, somehow, the self-confidence of the old man daunted him. It made him feel very young, and there is nothing so daunting to Youth as to feel young. Therefore he said, venerably, that he hoped Mr. Roberts realized that it was possible to deceive oneself in such matters. "It is a dangerous thing to neglect the means of grace," he said.

"Surely it is," said Henry Roberts, meekly; after which there was nothing for the caller to do but offer the Irvingite a copy of the *American Messenger* and take his departure. He was so genuinely concerned about Mr. Roberts's "danger," that he did not notice Philippa sitting on a stool at her father's side. But Philippa noticed him.

So, after their kind, did these two shepherds of souls endeavor to establish a relationship with Henry and Philippa Roberts. And they were equally successful. Philippa gave her apple blossoms to the old minister,—and went to Mr. Fenn's church the very next Sunday. Henry Roberts accepted the tracts with a simple belief in the kindly purpose of the young minister, and stayed away from both churches. But both father and daughter were pleased by the clerical attentions:

"I love Dr. Lavendar," Philippa said to her father.

"I am obliged to Mr. Fenn," her father said to Philippa. "The youth," he added, "cares for my soul. I am obliged to any one who cares for my soul."

He was, indeed, as Dr. Lavendar said, a man of humble mind; and yet with his humbleness was a serene certainty of belief as to his soul's welfare that would have been impossible to John Fenn, who measured every man's chance of salvation by his own theological yardstick, or even to Dr. Lavendar, who thought salvation unmeasurable. But then neither of these two ministers had had Henry Roberts's experience. It was very far back, that experience; it happened before Philippa was born; and when they came to live between the two villages Philippa was twenty-four years old....

It was in the thirties that young Roberts, a tanner in Lower Ripple, went to England to collect a small bequest left him by a relative. The sense of distance, the long weeks at sea in a sailing-vessel, the new country and the new people, all impressed themselves upon a very sensitive mind, a mind which, even without such emotional preparation, was ready to respond to any deeply emotional appeal. Then came the appeal. It was that new gospel of the Tongues, which, in those days, astounded and thrilled all London from the lips of Edward Irving—fanatic, saint, and martyr!—the man who, having prayed that God would speak again in prophecy, would not deny the power of prayer by refusing to believe that his prayer was answered, even though the prophecy was unintelligible. And later, when the passionate cadences of the spirit were in English, and were found to be only trite or foolish words, repeated and repeated in a wailing chant by some sincere, hysterical woman, he still believed that a new day of Pentecost had dawned upon a sinful world! "For," said he, "when I asked for bread, would God give me a stone?"

Henry Roberts went to hear the great preacher and forgot his haste to receive his little legacy so that he might hurry back to the tanyard. Irving's eloquence entranced him, and it alone would have held him longer than the time he had allowed himself for absence from the tannery. But it happened that he was present on that Lord's Day when, with a solemn and dreadful sound, the Tongues first spoke in that dingy Chapel in Regent Square, and no man who heard that Sound ever forgot it! The mystical youth from America was shaken to his very soul. He stayed on in London for nearly a year, immersing himself in those tides of emotion which swept saner minds than his from the somewhat dry land of ordinary human experience. That no personal revelation was made to him, that the searing benediction of the Tongues had not touched his own awed, uplifted brow, made no difference: he believed!—and prayed God to help any lingering unbelief that might be holding him back from deeper knowledges. To the end of his days he was Edward Irving's follower; and when he went back to America it was as a missionary of the new sect, that called itself by the sounding title of The Catholic Apostolic Church. In Lower Ripple he preached to any who would listen to him the doctrine of the new Pentecost. At first curiosity brought him hearers; his story of the Voice, dramatic and mysterious, was listened to in doubting silence; then disapproved of—so hotly disapproved of that he was sessioned and read out of Church.

But in those days in western Pennsylvania, mere living was too engrossing a matter for much thought of "tongues" and "voices"; it was easier, when a man talked of dreams and visions, not to argue with him, but to say that he was "crazy." So by and by Henry Roberts's heresy was forgotten and his religion merely smiled at. Certainly it struck no roots outside his own heart. Even his family did not share his belief. When he married, as he did when he was nearly fifty, his wife was impatient with his Faith—indeed, fearful of it, and with persistent, nagging reasonableness urged his return to the respectable paths of Presbyterianism. To his pain, when his girl, his Philippa, grew up she shrank from the emotion of his creed; she and her mother went to the brick church under the locust-trees of Lower Ripple; and when her mother died Philippa went there alone, for Henry Roberts, not being permitted to bear witness in the Church, did so out of it, by sitting at home on the Sabbath day, in a bare upper chamber, waiting for the manifestation of the Holy Spirit. It never came. The Tongues never spoke. Yet still, while the years passed, he waited, listening—listening—listening; a kindly, simple old man with mystical brown eyes, believing meekly in his own unworth to hear again that Sound from Heaven, as of a rushing, mighty wind, that had filled the London Chapel, bowing human souls before it as a great wind bows the standing corn!

It was late in the sixties that Henry Roberts brought this faith and his Philippa to the stone house on the Perryville pike, where, after some months had passed, they were discovered by the old and the young ministers. The two clergymen met once or twice in their calls upon the new-comer, and each acquired an opinion of the other: John Fenn said to himself that the old minister was a good man, if he was an Episcopalian; and Dr. Lavendar said to William King that he hoped there would be a match between the "theolog" and Philippa.

"The child ought to be married and have a dozen children," he said; "although Fenn's little sister will do to begin on—she needs mothering badly enough. Yes, Miss Philly ought to be making smearkase and apple-butter for that pale and excellent young man. He intimated that I was a follower of the Scarlet Woman because I wore a surplice."

"Now look here! I draw the line at that sort of talk," the doctor said; "he can lay down the law to me, all he wants to; but when it comes to instructing you—"

"Oh, well, he's young," Dr. Lavendar soothed him; "you can't expect him not to know everything at his age."

"He's a squirt," said William. In those days in Old Chester middle age was apt to sum up its opinion of youth in this expressive word.

"We were all squirts once," said Dr. Lavendar, "and very nice boys we were, too—at least I was. Yes, I hope the youngster will see what a sweet creature old Roberts's Philippa is."

She was a sweet creature; but as William King said, she was amusingly old-fashioned. The Old Chester girl of those days, who seems (to look back upon her in these days) so medieval, was modern compared to Philippa! But there was nothing mystical about her; she was just modest and full of pleasant silences and soft gaieties and simple, startling truth-telling. At first, when they came to live near Perryville, she used, when the weather was fine, to walk over the grassy road, under the brown and white branches of the sycamores, into Old Chester, to Dr. Lavendar's church. "I like to come to your church," she told him, "because you don't preach quite such long sermons as Mr. Fenn does." But when it rained or was very hot she chose the shorter walk and sat under John Fenn, looking up at his pale, ascetic face, lighted from within by his young certainties concerning the old ignorances of people like Dr. Lavendar—life and death and eternity. Of Dr. Lavendar's one certainty, Love, he was deeply ignorant, this honest boy, who was so concerned for Philippa's father's soul! But Philippa did not listen much to his certainties; she coaxed his little sister into her pew, and sat with the child cuddled up against her, watching her turn over the leaves of the hymn-book or trying to braid the fringe of Miss Philly's black silk mantilla into little pigtails. Sometimes Miss Philly would look up at the careworn young face in the pulpit and think how holy Mary's brother was, and how learned—and how shabby; for he had only a housekeeper, Mrs. Semple, to take care of him and Mary. Not but what he might have had somebody besides Mrs. Semple! Philippa, for all her innocence, could not help being aware that he might have had—almost anybody! For others of Philly's sex watched the rapt face there in the pulpit. When Philippa thought of that, a slow blush used to creep up to her very temples. She saw him oftener in the pulpit than out of it, because when he came to call on her father she was apt not to be present. At first he came very frequently to see the Irvingite, because he felt it his duty to "deal" with him; but he made so little impression that he foresaw the time when it would be necessary to say that Ephraim was joined to his idols. But though it might be right to "let him alone," he could not stop calling at Henry Roberts's house; "for," he reminded himself, "the believing daughter may sanctify the unbelieving father!" He said this once to Dr. Lavendar, when his roan and old Goliath met in a narrow lane and paused to let their masters exchange a word or two.

"But do you know what the believing daughter believes?" said Dr. Lavendar. He wiped his forehead with his red bandanna, for it was a hot day; then he put his old straw hat very far back on his head and looked at the young man with a twinkle in his eye, which, considering the seriousness of their conversation, was discomfiting; but, after all, as John Fenn reminded himself, Dr. Lavendar was very old, and so might be forgiven if his mind was lacking in seriousness. As for his question of what the daughter believed: "I think—I hope," said the young minister, "that she is sound. She comes to my church quite regularly." "But she comes to my church quite irregularly," Dr. Lavendar warned him; and there was another of those disconcerting twinkles.

The boy looked at him with honest, solemn eyes. "I still believe that she is sound," he said, earnestly.

Dr. Lavendar blew his nose with a flourish of the red bandanna. "Well, perhaps she is, perhaps she is," he said, gravely. But the reassurance of that "perhaps" did not make for John Fenn's peace of mind; he could not help asking himself whether Miss Philippa WAS a "believing daughter." She did not, he was sure, share her father's heresies, but perhaps she was indifferent to them? which would be a grievous thing! And certainly, as the old minister had declared, she did go "irregularly" to the Episcopal Church. John Fenn wished that he was sure of Miss Philippa's state of mind; and at last he said to himself that it was his duty to find out about it, so, with his little sister beside him, he started on a round of pastoral calls. He found Miss Philly sitting in the sunshine on the lowest step of the front porch—and it seemed to Mary that there was a good deal of delay in getting at the serious business of play; "for brother talks so much," she complained. But "brother" went on talking. He told Miss Philippa that he understood she went sometimes to Old Chester to church?

"Sometimes," she said.

"I do not mean," he said, hesitatingly, "to speak uncharitably, but we all know that Episcopacy is the handmaid of Papistry."

"Do we?" Philly asked, with grave eyes.

"Yes," said Mr. Fenn. "But even if Dr. Lavendar's teachings are defective,"—Mary plucked at his sleeve, and sighed loudly; "(no, Mary!)—even if his teachings are defective, he is a good man according to his lights; I am sure of that. Still, do you think it well to attend a place of worship when you cannot follow the pastor's teachings?"

"I love him. And I don't listen to what he says," she excused herself.

"But you should listen to what ministers say," the shocked young man protested—"at least to ministers of the right faith. But you should not go to church because you love ministers."

Philippa's face flamed. "I do not love—most of them."

Mary, leaning against the girl's knee, looked up anxiously into her face. "Do you love brother?" she said.

They were a pretty pair, the child and the girl, sitting there on the porch with the sunshine sifting down through the lacy leaves of the two big locusts on either side of the door. Philippa wore a pink and green palm-leaf chintz; it had six ruffles around the skirt and was gathered very full about her slender waist; her lips were red, and her cheeks and even her neck were delicately flushed; her red-brown hair was blowing all about her temples;

Mary had put an arm around her and was cuddling against her. Yes, even Mary's brother would have thought the two young things a pretty sight had there been nothing more serious to think of. But John Fenn's thoughts were so very serious that even Mary's question caused him no embarrassment; he merely said, stiffly, that he would like to see Miss Philippa alone. "You may wait here, Mary," he told his little sister, who frowned and sighed and went out to the gate to pull a handful of grass for the roan.

Philippa led her caller to her rarely used parlor, and sat down to listen in silent pallor to his exhortations. She made no explanations for not coming to his church regularly; she offered no excuse of filial tenderness for her indifference to her father's mistaken beliefs; she looked down at her hands, clasped tightly in her lap, then out of the window at the big roan biting at the hitching-post or standing very still to let Mary rub his silky nose. But John Fenn looked only at Philippa. Of her father's heresies he would not, he said, do more than remind her that the wiles of the devil against her soul might present them-selves through her natural affections; but in regard to her failure to wait upon the means of grace he spoke without mercy, for, he said, "faithful are the wounds of a friend."

"Are you my friend?" Philly asked, lifting her gray eyes suddenly.

Mr. Fenn was greatly confused; the text-books of the Western Seminary had not supplied him with the answer to such a question. He explained, hurriedly, that he was the friend of all who wished for salvation.

"I do not especially wish for it," Philippa said, very low.

For a moment John Fenn was silent with horror. "That one so young should be so hardened!" he thought; aloud, he bade her remember hell fire. He spoke with that sad and simple acceptance of the fact with which, even less than fifty years ago, men humbled themselves before the mystery which they had themselves created, of divine injustice. She must know, he said, his voice trembling with sincerity, that those who slighted the offers of grace were cast into outer darkness?

Philly said, softly, "Maybe."

"'Maybe?' Alas, it is, certainly! Oh, why, WHY do you absent yourself from the house of God?" he said, holding out entreating hands. Philippa made no reply. "Let us pray!" said the young man; and they knelt down side by side in the shadowy parlor. John Fenn lifted his harsh, melancholy face, gazing upward passionately, while he wrestled for her salvation; Philly, looking downward, tracing with a trembling finger the pattern of the beadwork on the ottoman before which she knelt, listened with an inward shiver of dismay and ecstasy. But when they rose to their feet she had nothing to say. He, too, was silent. He went away quite exhausted by his struggle with this impassive, unresisting creature.

He hardly spoke to Mary all the way home. "A hardened sinner," he was thinking. "Poor, lovely creature! So young and so lost!" Under Mary's incessant chatter, her tugs at the end of the reins, her little bursts of joy at the sight of a bird or a roadside flower, he was thinking, with a strange new pain—a pain no other sinner had ever roused in him—of the girl he had left. He knew that his arguments had not moved her. "I believe," he thought, the color rising in his face, "that she dislikes me! She says she loves Dr. Lavendar; yes, she must dislike me. Is my manner too severe? Perhaps my appearance is unattractive." He looked down at his coat uneasily.

As for Philly, left to herself, she picked up a bit of sewing, and her face, at first pale, grew slowly pink. "He only likes sinners," she thought; "and, oh, I am not a sinner!"

CHAPTER II

After that on Sabbath mornings Philippa sat with her father, in the silent upper chamber. At first Henry Roberts, listening—listening—for the Voice, thought, rapturously, that at the eleventh hour he was to win a soul—the most precious soul in his world!—to his faith. But when, after a while, he questioned her, he saw that this was not so; she stayed away from other churches, but not because she cared for his church. This troubled him, for the faith he had outgrown was better than no faith.

"Do you have doubts concerning the soundness of either of the ministers—the old man or the young man?" he asked her, looking at her with mild, anxious eyes.

"Oh no, sir," Philly said, smiling.

"Do you dislike them—the young man or the old man?"

"Oh no, father. I love—one of them."

"Then why not go to his church? Either minister can give you the seeds of salvation; one not less than the other. Why not sit under either ministry?"

"I don't know," Philippa said, faintly.

And indeed she did not know why she absented herself. She only knew two things: that the young man seemed to disapprove of the old man; and when she saw the young man in the pulpit, impersonal and holy, she suffered. Therefore she would not go to hear either man.

When Dr. Lavendar came to call upon her father, he used to glance at Philippa sometimes over his spectacles while Henry

Roberts was arguing about prophecies; but he never asked her why she stayed away from church; instead, he talked to her about John Fenn, and he seemed pleased when he heard that the young man was doing his duty in making pastoral calls. "And I—I, unworthy as I was!" Henry Roberts would say, "I heard the Voice, speaking through a sister's lips; and it said: Oh, sinner! for what, for what, what can separate, separate, from the love... Oh, nothing. Oh, nothing. Oh, nothing."

He would stare at Dr. Lavendar with parted lips. "I HEARD IT," he would say, in a whisper.

And Dr. Lavendar, bending his head gravely, would be silent for a respectful moment, and then he would look at Philippa. "You are teaching Fenn's sister to sew?" he would say. "Very nice! Very nice!"

Philly saw a good deal of the sister that summer; the young minister, recognizing Miss Philippa's fondness for Mary, and remembering a text as to the leading of a child, took pains to bring the little girl to Henry Roberts's door once or twice a week; and as August burned away into September Philippa's pleasure in her was like a soft wind blowing on the embers of her heart and kindling a flame for which she knew no name. She thought constantly of Mary, and had many small anxieties about her—her dress, her manners, her health; she even took the child into Old Chester one day to get William King to pull a little loose white tooth. Philly shook very much during the operation and mingled her tears with Mary's in that empty and bleeding moment that follows the loss of a tooth. She was so passionately tender with the little girl that the doctor told Dr. Lavendar that his match-making scheme seemed likely to prosper—"she's so fond of the sister, you should have heard her sympathize with the little thing!—that I think she will smile on the brother," he said.

"I'm afraid the brother hasn't cut his wisdom teeth yet," Dr. Lavendar said, doubtfully; "if he had, you might pull them, and she could sympathize with him; then it would all arrange itself. Well, he's a nice boy, a nice boy;—and he won't know so much when he gets a little older."

It was on the way home from Dr. King's that Philippa's feeling of responsibility about Mary brought her a sudden temptation. They were walking hand in hand along the road. The leaves on the mottled branches of the sycamores were thinning now, and the sunshine fell warm upon the two young things, who were still a little shaken from the frightful experience of tooth-pulling. The doctor had put the small white tooth in a box and gravely presented it to Mary, and now, as they walked along, she stopped sometimes to examine it and say, proudly, how she had "bleeded and bleeded!"

"Will you tell brother the doctor said I behaved better than the circus lion when his tooth was pulled?"

"Indeed I will, Mary!"

"An' he said he'd rather pull my tooth than a lion's tooth?"

"Of course I'll tell him."

"Miss Philly, shall I dream of my tooth, do you suppose?"

Philippa laughed and said she didn't know.

"I hope I will; it means something nice. I forget what, now."

"Dreams don't mean anything, Mary."

"Oh yes, they do!" the child assured her, skipping along with one arm round the girl's slender waist. "Mrs. Semple has a dream-book, and she reads it to me every day, an' she reads me what my dreams mean. Sometimes I haven't any dreams," Mary admitted, regretfully, "but she reads all the same. Did you ever dream about a black ox walking on its back legs? I never did. I don't want to. It means trouble."

"Goosey!" said Miss Philippa.

"If you dream of the moon," Mary went on, happily, "it means you are going to have a beau who'll love you."

"Little girls mustn't talk about love," Philippa said, gravely; but the color came suddenly into her face. To dream of the moon means—Why! but only the night before she had dreamed that she had been walking in the fields and had seen the moon rise over shocks of corn that stood against the sky like the plumed heads of Indian warriors! "Such things are foolish, Mary," Miss Philly said, her cheeks very pink. And while Mary chattered on about Mrs. Semple's book Philippa was silent, remembering how yellow the great flat disk of the moon had been in her dream; how it pushed up from behind the black edge of the world, and how, suddenly, the misty stubble-field was flooded with its strange light:—"you are going to have a beau!"

Philippa wished she might see the book, just to know what sort of things were read to Mary. "It isn't right to read them to the child," she thought; "it's a foolish book, Mary," she said, aloud. "I never saw such a book."

"I'll bring it the next time I come," Mary promised.

"Oh no, no," Philly said, a little breathlessly; "it's a wrong book. I couldn't read such a book, except—except to tell you how foolish and wrong it is."

Mary was not concerned with her friend's reasons; but she remembered to bring the ragged old book with her the very next time her brother dropped her at Mr. Roberts's gate to spend an hour with Miss Philippa. There had to be a few formal words between the preacher and the sinner before Mary had entire possession of her playmate, but when her brother drove away, promising to call for her later in the afternoon, she became so engrossed in the important task of picking hollyhock seeds that she quite forgot the dream-book. The air was hazy with autumn, and full of the scent of fallen leaves and dew-drenched grass and of the fresh tan-bark on the garden paths. On the other side of the road was a corn-field, where the corn stood in great shocks. Philly looked over at it, and drew a quick breath,—her dream!

"Did you bring that foolish book?" she said.

Mary, slapping her pocket, laughed loudly. "I 'most forgot! Yes, ma'am; I got it. I'll show what it says about the black ox—"

"No; you needn't," Miss Philly said; "you pick some more seeds for me, and I'll—just look at it." She touched the stained old book with shrinking fingertips; the moldering leather cover and the odor of soiled and thumb-marked leaves offended her. The first page was folded over, and when she spread it out, the yellowing paper cracked along its ancient creases; it was a map, with the signs of the Zodiac; in the middle was a single verse:

Mortal! Wouldst thou scan aright
Dreams and visions of the night?
Wouldst thou future secrets learn
And the fate of dreams discern?
Wouldst thou ope the Curtain dark
And thy future fortune mark?
Try the mystic page, and read
What the vision has decreed.

Philly, holding her red lip between her teeth, turned the pages:

"MONEY. TO DREAM OF FINDING MONEY; MOURNING AND LOSS.

"MONKEY. YOU HAVE SECRET ENEMIES.

"MOON." (Philippa shivered.) "A GOOD OMEN; IT DENOTES COMING JOY. GREAT SUCCESS IN LOVE."

She shut the book sharply, then opened it again. Such books sometimes told (so foolishly!) of charms which would bring love. She looked furtively at Mary; but the child, pulling down a great hollyhock to pick the fuzzy yellow disks, was not noticing Miss Philly's interest in the "foolish book." Philippa turned over the pages. Yes; the charms were there!...

Instructions for making dumb-cake, to cut which reveals a lover: "ANY NUMBER OF YOUNG FEMALES SHALL TAKE A HANDFUL OF WHEATEN FLOUR—" That was no use; there were too many females as it was!

"TO KNOW WHETHER A MAN SHALL HAVE THE WOMAN HE WISHES." Philippa sighed. Not that. A holy man does not "wish" for a woman.

"A CHARM TO CHARM A MAN'S LOVE." The blood suddenly ran tingling in Philly's veins. "LET A YOUNG MAID PICK OF ROSEMARY TWO ROOTS; OF MONK'S-HOOD—"

A line had been drawn through this last word, and another word written above it; but the ink was so faded, the page so woolly and thin with use, that it was impossible to decipher the correction; perhaps it was "mother-wort," an herb Philly did not know; or it might be "mandrake"? It looked as much like one as the other, the writing was so blurred and dim. "It is best to take what the book says," Philly said, simply; "besides, I haven't those other things in the garden, and I have monk's-hood and rosemary—if I should want to do it, just for fun."

"OF MONK'S-HOOD TWO ROOTS, AND OF THE FLOWER OF CORN TEN THREADS; LET HER SLEEP ON THEM ONE NIGHT. IN THE MORNING, LET HER SET THEM ON HER HEART AND WALK BACKWARDS TEN STEPS, PRAYING FOR THE LOVE OF HER BELOVED. LET HER THEN STEEP AND BOIL THESE THINGS IN FOUR GILLS OF PURE WATER ON WHICH THE MOON HAS SHONE FOR ONE NIGHT. WHEN SHE SHALL ADD THIS PHILTER TO THE DRINK OF THE ONE WHO LOVES HER NOT, HE SHALL LOVE THE FEMALE WHO MEETS HIS EYE FIRST AFTER THE DRINKING THEREOF. THEREFORE LET THE YOUNG MAID BE INDUSTRIOUS TO STAND BEFORE HIM WHEN HE SHALL DRINK IT."

"There is no harm in it," said Philly.

CHAPTER III

"Somebody making herb tea and stealing my business?" said William King, in his kindly voice; he had called to see old Hannah, who had been laid up for a day or two, and he stopped at the kitchen door to look in. Henry Roberts, coming from the sitting-room to join him, asked his question, too:

"What is this smell of herbs, Philippa? Are you making a drink for Hannah?" "Oh no, father," Philly said, briefly, her face very pink.

William King sniffed and laughed. "Ah, I see you don't give away your secrets to a rival," he said; and added, pleasantly, "but don't give your tea to Hannah without telling me what it is."

Miss Philippa said, dutifully, "Oh no, sir." But she did not tell him what the "tea" was, and certainly she offered none of it to old Hannah. All that day there was a shy joyousness about her, with sudden soft blushes, and once or twice a little half-frightened laugh; there was a puzzled look, too, in her face, as if she was not quite sure just what she was going to do, or rather, how she was going to do it. And, of course, that was the difficulty. How could she "add the philter to the drink of one who loved her not"?

Yet it came about simply enough. John Fenn had lately felt it borne in upon him that it was time to make another effort to deal with Henry Roberts; perhaps, he reasoned, to show concern about the father's soul might touch the daughter's hardened heart. It was when he reached this conclusion that he committed the extravagance of buying a new coat. So it happened that that very afternoon, while the house was still pungent with the scent of steeping herbs, he came to Henry Roberts's door, and knocked solemnly, as befitted his errand; (but as he heard her step in the hall he passed an anxious hand over a lapel of the new coat). Her father, she said, was not at home; would Mr. Fenn come in and wait for him? Mr. Fenn said he would. And as he always tried, poor boy! to be instant in season and out of season, he took the opportunity, while he waited for her father and she brought him a glass of wine and a piece of cake, to reprove her again for absence from church. But she was so meek that he found it hard to inflict those "faithful wounds" which should prove his friendship for her soul; she sat before him on the slippery horsehair sofa in the parlor, her hands locked tightly together in her lap, her eyes downcast, her voice very low and trembling. She admitted her backslidings: she acknowledged her errors; but as for coming to church—she shook her head:

"Please, I won't come to church yet."

"You mean you will come, sometime?"

"Yes; sometime."

"Behold, NOW is the accepted time!"

"I will come... afterwards."

"After what?" he insisted.

"After—" she said, and paused. Then suddenly lifted bold, guileless eyes: "After you stop caring for my soul."

John Fenn caught his breath. Something, he did not know what, seemed to jar him rudely from that pure desire for her salvation; he said, stumblingly, that he would ALWAYS care for her soul!—"for—for any one's soul." And was she quite well? His voice broke with tenderness. She must be careful to avoid the chill of these autumnal afternoons; "you are pale," he said, passionately—"don't—oh, don't be so pale!" It occurred to him that if she waited for him "not to care" for her salvation, she might die in her sins; die before coming to the gate of heaven, which he was so anxious to open to her!

Philippa did not see his agitation; she was not looking at him. She only said, softly, "Perhaps you will stay to tea?"

He answered quickly that he would be pleased to do so. In the simplicity of his saintly egotism it occurred to him that the religious pleasure of entertaining him might be a means of grace to her. When she left him in the dusk of the chilly room to go and see to the supper, he fell into silent prayer for the soul that did not desire his care.

Henry Roberts, summoned by his daughter to entertain the guest until supper was ready, found him sitting in the darkness of the parlor; the old man was full of hospitable apologies for his Philippa's forgetfulness; "she did not remember the lamp!" he lamented; and making his way through the twilight of the room, he took off the prism-hung shade of the tall astral lamp on the center-table, and fumbled for a match to light the charred and sticky wick; there were very few occasions in this plain household when it was worth while to light the best lamp! This was one of them, for in those days the office dignified the man to a degree that is hardly understood now. But Henry Roberts's concern was not entirely a matter of social propriety; it was a desire to propitiate this young man who was living in certain errors of belief, so that he would be in a friendly attitude of mind and open to the arguments which were always burning on the lips of Edward Irving's follower. He did not mean to begin them until they were at supper; so he and John Fenn sat in silence waiting Philippa's summons to the dining-room. Neither of them had any small talk; Mr. Roberts was making sure that he could trust his memory to repeat those wailing cadences of the Voice, and John Fenn, still shaken by something he could not understand that had been hidden in what he understood too well—a sinner's indifference to grace—was trying to get back to his serene, impersonal arrogance.

As for Philippa, she was frightened at her temerity in having invited the minister to a Hannahless supper; her flutter of questions as to "what" and "how" brought the old woman from her bed, in spite of the girl's half-hearted protests that she "mustn't think of getting up! Just tell me what to do," she implored, "I can manage. We are going to have—TEA!"

"We always have tea," Hannah said, sourly; yet she was not really sour, for, like William King and Dr. Lavendar, Hannah had discerned possibilities in the Rev. John Fenn's pastoral visits. "Get your Sunday-go-to-meeting dress on," she commanded, hunching a shawl over a rheumatic shoulder and motioning the girl out of the kitchen.

Philippa, remorseful and breathless, ran quickly up to her room to put on her best frock, smooth her shining hair down in two loops over her ears, and pin her one adornment, a flat gold brooch, on the bosom of her dress. She lifted her candle and looked at herself in the black depths of the little swinging glass on her high bureau, and her face fell into sudden wistful lines. "Oh, I do not look wicked," she thought, despairingly.

John Fenn, glancing at her across the supper-table, had some such thought himself; how strange that one who was so perverted in belief should not betray perversion in her countenance. "On the contrary, her face is pleasing," he said, simply. He feared, noticing the brooch, that she was vain, as well as indifferent to her privileges; he wondered if she had observed his new coat.

Philippa's vanity did not, at any rate, give her much courage; she scarcely spoke, except to ask him whether he took cream and sugar in his tea. When she handed his cup to him, she said, very low, "Will you taste it, and see if it is right?"

He was so conscious of the tremor of her voice and hand that he made haste to reassure her, sipping his tea with much politeness of manner; as he did so, she said, suddenly, and with compelling loudness, "Is it—agreeable?"

John Fenn, startled, looked at her over the rim of his cup. "Very; very indeed," he said, quickly. But he instantly drank some water. "It is, perhaps, a little strong," he said, blinking. Then, having qualified his politeness for conscience' sake, he drank all the bitter tea for human kindness' sake—for evidently Miss Philippa had taken pains to give him what he might like. After that she did not speak, but her face grew very rosy while she sat in silence listening to her father and their guest. Henry Roberts forgot to eat, in the passion of his theological arguments, but as supper proceeded he found his antagonist less alert than usual; the minister defended his own doctrines instead of attacking those of his host; he even admitted, a little listlessly, that if the Power fell upon him, if he himself spoke in a strange tongue, then perhaps he would believe—"that is, if I could be sure I was not out of my mind at the time," he qualified, dully. Philippa took no part in the discussion; it would not have been thought becoming in her to do so; but indeed, she hardly heard what the two men were saying. She helped old Hannah carry away the dishes, and then sat down by the table and drew the lamp near her so that she could sew; she sat there smiling a little, dimpling even, and looking down at her seam; she did not notice that John Fenn was being worsted, or that once he failed altogether to reply, and sat in unprotesting silence under Henry Roberts's rapt remembrances. A curious blackness had settled under his eyes, and twice he passed his hand across his lips.

"They are numb," he said, in surprised apology to his host. A moment later he shivered violently, beads of sweat burst out on his forehead, and the color swept from his face. He started up, staring wildly about him; he tried to speak, but his words stumbled into incoherent babbling. It was all so sudden, his rising, then falling back into his chair, then slipping sidewise and crumpling up upon the floor, all the while stammering unmeaning words—that Henry Roberts sat looking at him in dumb amazement. It was Philippa who cried out and ran forward to help him, then stopped midway, her hands clutched together at her throat, her eyes dilating with a horror that seemed to paralyze her so that she was unable to move to his assistance. The shocked silence of the moment was broken by Fenn's voice, trailing on and on, in totally unintelligible words.

Henry Roberts, staring open-mouthed, suddenly spoke: "The VOICE!" he said. But Philippa, as though she were breaking some invisible bond that held her, groaning even with the effort of it, said, in a whisper: "No. Not that. He is dying. Don't you see? That's what it is. He is dying."

Her father, shocked from his ecstasy, ran to John Fenn's side, trying to lift him and calling upon him to say what was the matter.

"He is going to die," said Philippa, monotonously.

Henry Roberts, aghast, calling loudly to old Hannah, ran to the kitchen and brought back a great bowl of hot water. "Drink it!" he said. "Drink it, I tell ye! I believe you're poisoned!"

And while he and Hannah bent over the unconscious young man, Philippa seemed to come out of her trance; slowly, with upraised hands, and head bent upon her breast, she stepped backward, backward, out of the room, out of the house. On the doorstep, in the darkness, she paused and listened for several minutes to certain dreadful sounds in the house. Then, suddenly, a passion of purpose swept the daze of horror away.

"HE SHALL NOT DIE," she said.

She flung her skirt across her arm that her feet might not be hampered, and fled down the road toward Old Chester. It was very dark. At first her eyes, still blurred with the lamplight, could not distinguish the footpath, and she stumbled over the grassy border into the wheel-ruts; then, feeling the loose dust under her feet, she ran and ran and ran. The blood began to sing in her ears; once her throat seemed to close so that she could not breathe, and for a moment she had to walk,—but her hands, holding up her skirts, trembled with terror at the delay. The road was very dark under the sycamore-trees; twice she tripped and fell into the brambles at one side or against a gravelly bank on the other. But stumbling somehow to her feet, again she ran and ran and ran. The night was very still; she could hear her breath tearing her throat; once she felt something hot and salty in her mouth; it was then she had to stop and walk for a little space—she must walk or fall down! And she could not fall down, no! no! no! he would die if she fell down! Once a figure loomed up in the haze, and she caught the glimmer of an inquisitive eye. "Say," a man's voice said, "where are you bound for?" There was something in the tone that gave her a stab of fright; for a minute or two her feet seemed to fly, and she heard a laugh behind her in the darkness: "What's your hurry?" the voice called after her. And still she ran. But she was saying to herself that she must STOP; she must stand still just for a moment. "Oh, just for a minute?" her body whimperingly entreated; she would not listen to it! She must not listen, even though her heart burst with the strain. But her body had its way, and she fell into a walk, although she was not aware of it. In a gasping whisper she was saying, over and over: "Doctor, hurry; he'll die; hurry; I killed him." She tried to be silent, but her lips moved mechanically. "Doctor, hurry; he'll—Oh, I MUSTN'T talk!" she told herself, "it takes my breath"—but still her lips moved. She began to run, heavily. "I can't talk—if—I—run—" It was then that she saw a glimmer of light and knew that she was almost in Old Chester.

Very likely she would have fallen if she had not seen that far-off window just when she did.

At William King's house she dropped against the door, her fingers still clinging to the bell. She was past speaking when the doctor lifted her and carried her into the office. "No; don't try to tell me what it is," he said; "I'll put Jinny into the buggy, and we'll get back in a jiffy. I understand; Hannah is worse."

"Not... Hannah—"

"Your father?" he said, picking up his medicine-case.

"Not father; Mr.—Fenn—"

As the doctor hurried out to the stable to hitch up he bade his wife put certain remedies into his bag,—"and look after that child," he called over his shoulder to his efficient Martha. She was so efficient that when he had brought Jinny and the buggy to the door, Philly was able to gasp out that Mr. Fenn was sick. "Dying."

"Don't try to talk," he said again, as he helped her into the buggy. But after a while she was able to tell him, hoarsely:

"I wanted him to love me." William King was silent. "I used a charm. It was wicked."

"Come, come; not wicked," said the doctor; "a little foolish, perhaps. A new frock, and a rose in your hair, and a smile at another man, would be enough of a charm, my dear."

Philippa shook her head. "It was not enough. I wore my best frock, and I went to Dr. Lavendar's church—"

"Good gracious!" said William King.

"They were not enough. So I used a charm. I made a drink—"

"Ah!" said the doctor, frowning. "What was in the drink, Miss Philly?"

"Perhaps it was not the right herb," she said; "it may have been 'mother-wort'; but the book said 'monk's-hood,' and I—"

William King reached for his whip and cut Jinny across the flanks. "ACONITE!" he said under his breath, while Jinny leaped forward in shocked astonishment.

"Will he live?" said Philippa. Dr. King, flecking Jinny again, and letting his reins hang over the dashboard, could not help putting a comforting arm around her. "I hope so," he said; "I hope so!" After all, there was no use telling the child that probably by this time her lover was either dead or getting better. "It's his own fault," William King thought, angrily. "Why in thunder didn't he fall in love like a man, instead of making the child resort to—G'on, Jinny! G'on!" He still had the whip in his hand when they drew up at the gate.

CHAPTER IV

When Philippa Roberts had fled out into the night for help, her father and old Hannah were too alarmed to notice her absence. They went hurrying back and forth with this remedy and that. Again and again they were ready to give up; once Henry Roberts said, "He is gone!" and once Hannah began to cry, and said, "Poor lad, poor boy!" Yet each made one more effort, their shadows looming gigantic against the walls or stretching across the ceiling, bending and sinking as they knelt beside the poor young man, who by that time was beyond speech. So the struggle went on. But little by little life began to gain. John Fenn's eyes opened. Then he smiled. Then he said something-they could not hear what.

"Bless the Lord!" said Henry Roberts.

"He's asking for Philly," said old Hannah. By the time the doctor and Philippa reached the house the shadow of death had lifted.

"It must have been poison," Mr. Roberts told the doctor. "When he gets over it he will tell us what it was."

"I don't believe he will," said William King; he was holding Fenn's wrist between his firm fingers, and then he turned up a fluttering eyelid and looked at the still dulled eye.

Philippa, kneeling on the other side of John Fenn, said loudly: "I will tell HIM—and perhaps God will forgive me."

The doctor, glancing up at her, said: "No, you won't—anyhow at present. Take that child up-stairs, Hannah," he commanded, "and put her to bed. She ran all the way to Old Chester to get me," he explained to Henry Roberts.

Before he left the house that night he sat for a few minutes at Philippa's bedside. "My dear little girl," he said, in his kind, sensible voice, "the best thing to do is to forget it. It was a foolish thing to do—that charm business; but happily no harm is done. Now say nothing about it, and never do it again."

Philippa turned her shuddering face away. "Do it again? OH!"

As William King went home he apologized to Jinny for that cut across her flanks by hanging the reins on the overhead hook, and letting her plod along at her own pleasure. He was saying to himself that he hoped he had done right to tell the child to hold her tongue. "It was just tomfoolery," he argued; "there was no sin about it, so confession wouldn't do her any good; on the contrary, it would hurt a girl's self-respect to have a man know she had tried to catch him. But what a donkey he was not to see.... Oh yes; I'm sure I'm right," said William King. "I wonder how Dr. Lavendar would look at it?"

Philippa, at any rate, was satisfied with his advice. Perhaps the story of what she had done might have broken from her pale lips had her father asked any questions; but Henry Roberts had retreated into troubled silence. There had been one wonderful moment when he thought that at last his faith was to be justified and by the unbeliever himself! and he had cried out, with a passion deferred for more than thirty years: "The VOICE!" But behold, the voice, babbling and meaningless, was nothing but sickness. No one could guess what the shock of that disappointment was. He was not able even to speak of it. So Philippa was asked no awkward questions, and her self-knowledge burned deep into her heart.

In the next few days, while the minister was slowly recovering in the great four-poster in Henry Roberts's guest-room, she listened to Hannah's speculations as to the cause of his attack, and expressed no opinion. She was dumb when John Fenn tried to tell her how grateful he was to her for that terrible run through the darkness for his sake.

"You should not be grateful," she said, at last, in a whisper.

But he was grateful; and, furthermore, he was very happy in those days of slow recovery. The fact was that that night, when he had been so near death, he had heard Philippa, in his first dim moments of returning consciousness, stammering out those distracted words: "Perhaps God will forgive me." To John Fenn those words meant the crowning of all his efforts: she had repented!

"Truly," he said, lying very white and feeble on his pillow and looking into Philly's face when she brought him his gruel, "truly,

> "He moves in a mysterious way
> His wonders to perform!"

The "mysterious way" was the befalling of that terrible illness in Henry Roberts's house, so that Philippa should be impressed by it. "If my affliction has been blessed to any one else, I am glad to have suffered it," he said.

Philippa silently put a spoonful of gruel between his lips; he swallowed it as quickly as he could. "I heard you call upon God for forgiveness; the Lord is merciful and gracious!"

Philly said, very low, "Yes; oh YES." So John Fenn thanked God and took his gruel, and thought it was very good. He thought, also, that Miss Philippa was very good to be so good to him. In those next few days, before he was strong enough to be moved back to his own house, he thought more of her goodness and less of her salvation. It was then that he had his great moment, his revealing moment! All of a sudden, at the touch of Life, his honest artificiality had dropped from him, and he knew that he had never before known anything worth knowing! He knew he was in love. He knew it when he realized that he was not in the least troubled about her soul. "That is what she meant!" he thought; "she wanted me to care for her, before I cared for her soul." He was so simple in his acceptance of the revelation that she loved him, that when he went to ask her to be his wife the blow of her reply almost knocked him back into his ministerial affectations:

"No."

When John Fenn got home that evening he went into his study and shut the door. Mary came and pounded on it, but he only said, in a muffled voice:

"No, Mary. Not now. Go away."

He was praying for resignation to what he told himself was the will of God. "The Lord is unwilling that my thoughts should be diverted from His service by my own personal happiness." Then he tried to put his thoughts on that service by deciding upon a text for his next sermon. But the texts which suggested themselves were not steadying to his bewildered mind:

"LOVE ONE ANOTHER." ("I certainly thought she loved me.")

"MARVEL NOT, MY BRETHREN, IF THE WORLD HATE YOU." ("I am, perhaps, personally unattractive to her; and yet I wonder why?") He was not a conceited man; but, like all his sex, he really did "marvel" a little at the lack of feminine appreciation. He marveled so much that a week later he took Mary and walked out to Mr. Roberts's house. This time Mary, to her disgust, was left with Miss Philly's father, while her brother and Miss Philly walked in the frosted garden. Later, when that walk was over, and the little sister trudged along at John Fenn's side in the direction of Perryville, she was very fretful because he would not talk to her. He was occupied, poor boy, in trying again not to "marvel," and to be submissive to the divine will.

After that, for several months, he refused Mary's plea to be taken to visit Miss Philly. He had, he told himself, "submitted"; but submission left him very melancholy and solemn, and also a little resentful; indeed, he was so low in his mind, that once he threw out a bitter hint to Dr. Lavendar,—who, according to his wont, put two and two together.

"Men in our profession, sir," said John Fenn, "must not expect personal happiness."

"Well," said Dr. Lavendar, meditatively, "perhaps if we don't expect it, the surprise of getting it makes it all the better. I expected it; but I've exceeded my expectations!"

"But you are not married," the young man said, impulsively.

Dr. Lavendar's face changed; "I hope you will marry, Fenn," he said, quietly. At which John Fenn said, "I am married to my profession; that is enough for any minister."

"You'll find your profession a mighty poor housekeeper," said Dr. Lavendar.

It was shortly after this that Mr. Fenn and his big roan broke through the snow-drifts and made their way to Henry Roberts's house. "I must speak to you alone, sir," he said to the Irvingite, who, seeing him approaching, had hastened to open the door for him and draw him in out of the cold sunshine.

What the caller had to say was brief and to the point: Why was his daughter so unkind? John Fenn did not feel now that the world—which meant Philippa—hated him. He felt—he could not help feeling—that she did not even dislike him; "on the contrary...." So what reason had she for refusing him? But old Mr. Roberts shook his head. "A young female does not have 'reasons,'" he said. But he was sorry for the youth, and he roused himself from his abstraction long enough to question his girl:

"He is a worthy young man, my Philippa. Why do you dislike him?"

"I do not dislike him."

"Then why—?" her father protested.

But Philly was silent.

Even Hannah came to the rescue:

"You'll get a crooked stick at the end, if you don't look out!"

Philly laughed; then her face fell. "I sha'n't have any stick, ever!"

And Hannah, in her concern, confided her forebodings about the stick to Dr. King.

"I wonder," William said to himself, uneasily, "if I was wise to tell that child to hold her tongue? Perhaps they might have straightened it out between 'em before this, if she had told him and been done with it. I've a great mind to ask Dr. Lavendar."

He did ask him; at first with proper precautions not to betray a patient's confidence, but, at a word from Dr. Lavendar, tumbling into truthfulness.

"You are talking about young Philippa Roberts?" Dr. Lavendar announced, calmly, when William was half-way through his story of concealed identities.

"How did you guess it?" the doctor said, astonished; "oh, well, yes, I am. I guess there's no harm telling you—" "Not the slightest," said Dr. Lavendar, "especially as I knew it already from the young man—I mean, I knew she wouldn't have him. But I didn't know why until your story dovetailed with his. William, the thing has festered in her! The lancet ought to have been used the next day. I believe she'd have been married by this time if she'd spoken out, then and there."

William King was much chagrined. "I thought, being a girl, you know, her pride, her self-respect—"

"Oh yes; the lancet hurts," Dr. Lavendar admitted; "but it's better than—well, I don't know the terms of your trade, Willy-but I guess you know what I mean?"

"I guess I do," said William King, thoughtfully. "Do you suppose it's too late now?"

"It will be more of an operation," Dr. Lavendar conceded.

"Could I tell him?" William said, after a while.

"I don't see why not," Dr. Lavendar said.

"I suppose I'd have to ask her permission?"

"Nonsense!" said Dr. Lavendar.

That talk between the physician of the soul and the physician of the body happened on the very night when John Fenn, in his study in Perryville, with Mary dozing on his knee, threw over, once and for all, what he had called "submission" and made up his mind to get his girl! The very next morning he girded himself and walked forth upon the Pike toward Henry Roberts's house. He did not take Mary with him,—but not because he meant to urge salvation on Miss Philly! As it happened, Dr. King, too, set out upon the Perryville road that morning, remarking to Jinny that if he had had his wits about him that night in November, she would have been saved the trip on this May morning. The trip was easy enough; William had found a medical pamphlet among his mail, and he was reading it, with the reins hanging from the crook of his elbow. It was owing to this method of driving that John Fenn reached the Roberts house before Jinny passed it, so she went all the way to Perryville, and then had to turn round to follow on his track.

"Brother went to see Miss Philly, and he wouldn't take me," Mary complained to William King, when he drew up at the minister's door; and the doctor was sympathetic to the extent of five cents for candy comfort.

But when Jinny reached the Roberts gate Dr. King saw John Fenn down in the garden with Philippa. "Ho-ho!" said William. "I guess I'll wait and see if he works out his own salvation." He hitched Jinny, and went in to find Philippa's father, and to him he freed his mind. The two men sat on the porch looking down over the tops of the lilac-bushes into the garden, where they could just see the heads of the two young, unhappy people.

"It's nonsense, you know," said William King, "that Philly doesn't take that boy. He's head over heels in love with her."

"She is not attached to him in any such manner," Henry Roberts said; "I wonder a little at it, myself. He is a good youth."

The doctor looked at him wonderingly; it occurred to him that if he had a daughter he would understand her better than Philly's father understood her. "I think the child cares for him," he said; then, hesitatingly, he referred to John Fenn's sickness. "I suppose you know about it?" he said.

Philly's father bent his head; he knew, he thought, only too well; no divine revelation in a disordered digestion!

"Don't you think," William King said, smiling, "you might try to make her feel that she is wrong not to accept him, now that the charm has worked, so to speak?"

"The charm?" the old man repeated, vaguely.

"I thought you understood," the doctor said, frowning; then, after a minute's hesitation, he told him the facts.

Henry Roberts stared at him, shocked and silent; his girl, his Philippa, to have done such a thing! "So great a sin—my little Philly!" he said, faintly. He was pale with distress.

"My dear sir," Dr. King protested, impatiently, "don't talk about SIN in connection with that child. I wish I'd held my tongue!"

Henry Roberts was silent. Philippa's share in John Fenn's mysterious illness removed it still further from that revelation, waited for during all these years with such passionate patience. He paid no attention to William King's reassurances; and his silence was so silencing that by and by the doctor stopped talking and looked down into the garden again. He observed that those two heads had not drawn any nearer together. It was not John Fenn's fault....

"There can be no good reason," he was saying to Philippa. "If it is a bad reason, I will overcome it! Tell me why?"

She put her hand up to her lips and trembled.

"Come," he said; "it is my due, Philippa. I WILL know!"

Philippa shook her head. He took her other hand and stroked it, as one might stroke a child's hand to comfort and encourage it.

"You must tell me, beloved," he said. Philippa looked at him with scared eyes; then, suddenly pulling her hands from his and turning away, she covered her face and burst into uncontrollable sobbing. He, confounded and frightened, followed her and tried to soothe her.

"Never mind, Philly, never mind! if you don't want to tell me— "

"I do want to tell you. I will tell you! You will despise me. But I will tell you. I DID A WICKED DEED. It was this very plant-here, where we stand, monk's-hood! It was poison. I didn't know—oh, I didn't know. The book said monk's-hood—it was a mistake. But I did a wicked deed. I tried to kill you— "

She swayed as she spoke, and then seemed to sink down and down, until she lay, a forlorn little heap, at his feet. For one dreadful moment he thought she had lost her senses. He tried to lift her, saying, with agitation:

"Philly! We will not speak of it— "

"I murdered you," she whispered. "I put the charm into your tea, to make you... love me. You didn't die. But it was murder. I meant—I meant no harm— "

He understood. He lifted her up and held her in his arms. Up on the porch William King saw that the two heads were close together!

"Why!" the young man said. "Why—but Philly! You loved me!"

"What difference does that make?" she said, heavily.

"It makes much difference to me," he answered; he put his hand on her soft hair and tried to press her head down again on his shoulder. But she drew away.

"No; no."

"But— " he began. She interrupted him.

"Listen," she said; and then, sometimes in a whisper, sometimes breaking into a sob, she told him the story of that November night. He could hardly hear it through.

"Love, you loved me! You will marry me."

"No; I am a wicked girl—a—a—an immodest girl— "

"My beloved, you meant no wrong—" He paused, seeing that she was not listening.

Her father and the doctor were coming down the garden path; William King, beaming with satisfaction at the proximity of those two heads, had summoned Henry Roberts to "come along and give 'em your blessing!"

But as he reached them, standing now apart, the doctor's smile faded—evidently something had happened. John Fenn, tense with distress, called to him with frowning command: "Doctor! Tell her, for heaven's sake, tell her that it was nothing—that charm! Tell her she did no wrong."

"No one can do that," Henry Roberts said; "it was a sin."

"Now, look here—" Dr. King began.

"It was a sin to try to move by foolish arts the will of God."

Philippa turned to the young man, standing quivering beside her. "You see?" she said.

"No! No, I don't see—or if I do, never mind."

Just for a moment her face cleared. (Yes, truly, he was not thinking of her soul now!) But the gleam faded. "Oh, father, I am a great sinner," she whispered.

"No, you're not!" William King said.

"Yes, my Philippa, you are," Henry Roberts agreed, solemnly.

The lover made a despairing gesture: "Doctor King! tell her 'no!' 'no!'"

"Yes," her father went on, "it was a sin. Therefore, Philippa, SIN NO MORE. Did you pray that this young man's love might be given to you?"

Philippa said, in a whisper, "Yes."

"And it was given to you?"

"Yes."

"Philippa, was it the foolish weed that moved him to love?" She was silent. "My child, my Philly, it was your Saviour who moved the heart of this youth, because you asked Him. Will you do such despite to your Lord as to reject the gift he has given in answer to your prayer?" Philippa, with parted lips, was listening intently: "The gift He had given!"

Dr. King dared not speak. John Fenn looked at him, and then at Philippa, and trembled. Except for the sound of a bird stirring in its nest overhead in the branches, a sunny stillness brooded over the garden. Then, suddenly, the stillness was shattered by a strange sound—a loud, cadenced chant, full of rhythmical repetitions. The three who heard it thrilled from head to foot; Henry Roberts did not seem to hear it: it came from his own lips.

"Oh, Philippa! Oh, Philippa! I do require—I do require that you accept your Saviour's gift. Add not sin to sin. Oh, add not sin to sin by making prayer of no avail! Behold, He has set before thee an open door. Oh, let no man shut it. Oh, let no man shut it...."

The last word fell into a low, wailing note. No one spoke. The bird rustled in the leaves above them; a butterfly wavered slowly down to settle on a purple flag in the sunshine. Philly's eyes filled with blessed tears. She stretched out her arms to her father and smiled. But it was John Fenn who caught those slender, trembling arms against his breast; and, looking over at the old man, he said, softly, "THE VOICE OF GOD."

... "and I," said William King, telling the story that night to Dr. Lavendar—"I just wanted to say 'the voice of COMMON SENSE!'"

"My dear William," said the old man, gently, "the most beautiful thing in the world is the knowledge that comes to you, when you get to be as old as I am, that they are the same thing."

www.ingramcontent.com/pod-product-compliance
Lightning Source LLC
LaVergne TN
LVHW101933220826
846093LV00009B/447

* 9 7 8 9 3 5 4 7 8 7 8 6 7 *